ISAAC NEWTON INVENTED THE CALCULUS AND DISCOVERED
THE LAWS THAT GOVERN GRAVITY.

ALBERT EINSTEIN'S MATHEMATICS HELPED UNLOCK
THE SECRETS OF THE ATOM.

Mathematics

By Irving Adler
Illustrated by Ron Miller

 Doubleday
NEW YORK LONDON TORONTO SYDNEY AUCKLAND

To Joyce

Published by Doubleday, a division of
Bantam Doubleday Dell
Publishing Group, Inc.
666 Fifth Avenue, New York,
New York 10103

Doubleday and the portrayal of an anchor
with a dolphin are trademarks of
Doubleday, a division of Bantam Doubleday
Dell Publishing Group, Inc.

Library of Congress
Cataloging-in-Publication Data

Adler, Irving.
    Mathematics / by Irving Adler :
illustrated by Ron Miller.—1st ed.
       p. cm.
    Includes index.
    Summary: An introduction to the
science of numbers and space, discussing
basic concepts, and including an
introduction to computer programming,
mathematical games, and activities.
    1. Mathematics—Juvenile
literature. {1. Mathematics.} I. Miller,
Ron, 1947–   . II. Title.
QA40.5.A3   1990
510—dc20   89-32712   CIP AC

RL: 3.1

ISBN 0-385-26142-X
ISBN 0-385-26143-8   (lib. bdg.)
Illustrations copyright © 1990 by Ron Miller
Text copyright © 1990 by Irving Adler

The following was reproduced with permission from
The Museum of Modern Art: *Composition in White,
Black and Red* by Piet Mondrian, 1936. Oil on canvas,
40¼″ x 41,″ Collection, The Museum of Modern Art,
New York. Gift of Advisory Committee.

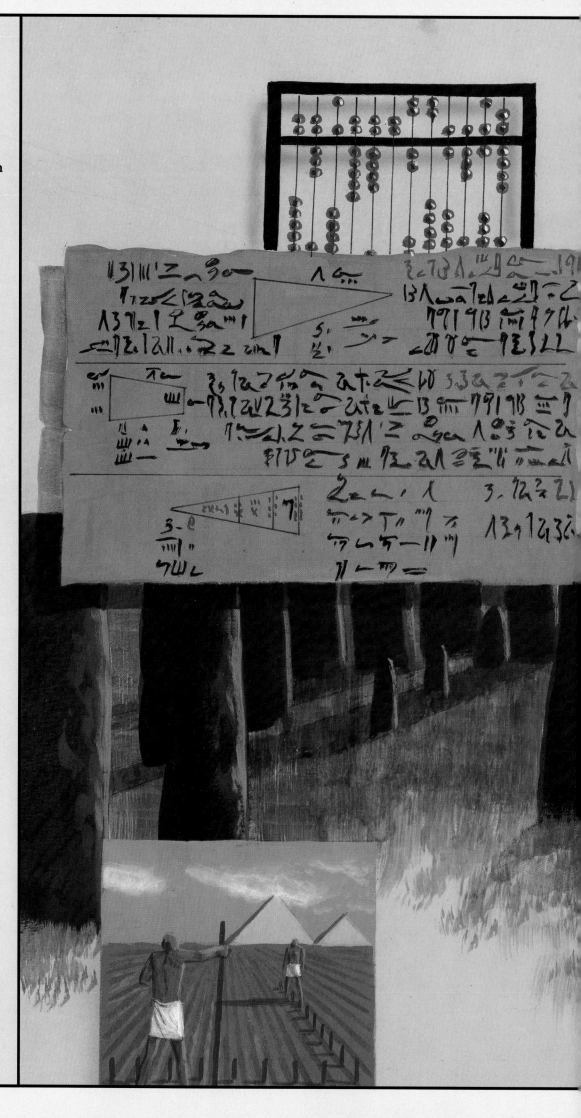

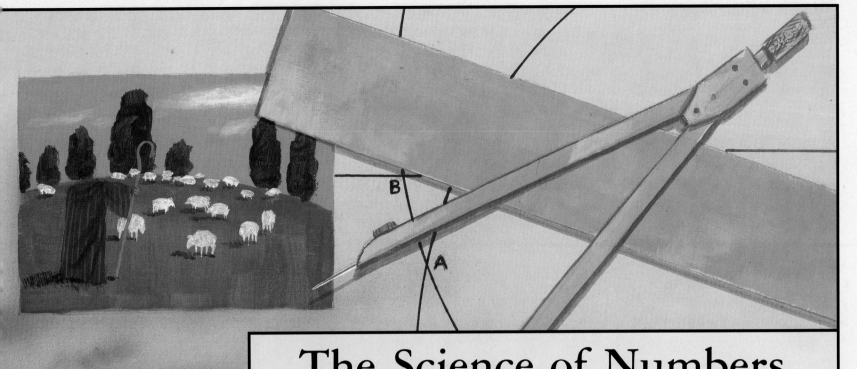

The Science of Numbers and Space

Mathematics is the science in which we think carefully about numbers and space. It developed along with civilization to help men and women solve practical problems. But people also found numbers and shapes in space interesting in themselves and began to play with them for fun.

Over ten thousand years ago all people got their food by hunting and by gathering wild fruits and berries. To keep track of their supplies they learned how to *count*, using the *natural numbers*, 1, 2, 3, 4, and so on. Later, when people became farmers and shepherds, they invented the crafts of pottery and basketry to make containers for storing things, spinning and weaving for making cloth, and smelting and forging of metals to make tools and weapons. Carpenters and masons built homes for the people, palaces for their rulers, and great tombs like the pyramids for their dead kings. Commerce developed for the exchange of products, and money was invented.

In these activities counting became even more important, and people also had to learn how to *measure* and *calculate*. For measuring they sometimes had to use *fractions*, and to calculate, they learned how to add, subtract, multiply, and divide. *Arithmetic* began to grow. Measuring land made it necessary to learn about the sizes and shapes of fields, and the subject of *geometry*, which studies space, was created.

1234567

Climbing the
Number Ladder

To count we use the natural numbers, 1, 2, 3, 4, and so on. The natural numbers are like a ladder that has a bottom and no top. The first rung of the ladder is the number 1. The next rung above it is the number 2. As you climb from rung to rung, you reach higher and higher numbers. Since there is no highest number, the ladder never ends.

On a hand calculator you can display the natural numbers in their proper order, starting with 1, without using any number key except 1. A number ladder can help illustrate this. Press the key for 1 on the calculator, and it displays the number 1. This puts you on the first rung of the number ladder. To get to 2, you have to go up one rung. This means you *add one*. On the calculator press the keys +, 1, and =. The calculator then displays the number 2. To get from 2 to 3, you add one again, so again press the keys +, 1, =. If you repeat this process over and over, the calculator will display the natural numbers in their proper order. Press $1 + 1 = + 1 = + 1 = + 1 =$ and so on forever.

Instead of repeating the sequence $+ 1 =$ over and over again forever, we can give the same information in a short way by writing $+ 1 =$ only once and then drawing an arrow from the = to the + to show that you go back to repeat that sequence: $1 + 1 =$

We can also instruct a *computer* to count by printing the natural numbers on the screen in their proper order. By learning how to do this you will begin to learn *computer programming* in the computer language called BASIC.

To prepare a computer for using BASIC, turn it on and put in the disc with the operating system. Then when the computer announces that it is ready, type BASIC, and press the ENTER key, the key that has a curved arrow on it. (Skip this step in an Apple computer.)

A computer program is a set of instructions to the computer that it stores in its memory and then reads and follows when it is told to do so. The instructions are numbered so that the computer knows the order in which the instructions are to be followed. But instead of numbering the instructions 1, 2, 3, and so on, it is usual to number the steps 10, 20, 30, etc. This makes it possible to insert a step without renumbering the whole program. Suppose, for example, you decide that you need a new step between step 10 and step 20. The computer will automatically put the new step in its right place if you call it step 15.

The first thing we have to do is give a name to the numbers that we want the computer to print. We use a letter of the alphabet for this name. Let's use the letter N. We also have to tell the computer the first number that this letter will stand for. Since the first number we want printed is 1, the first step of the program is: 10 N = 1

To get the computer to store this instruction in its memory, we press the ENTER key. Press the ENTER key after you finish typing each of the remaining numbered steps in the program. Now that the computer knows what number we want it to print first, we have to tell it to print it. So the next instruction is: 20 PRINT N

Now we want the computer to start climbing the number ladder. We want it to change the number in its memory to the next higher number. From what we have done with the hand calculator, we know that we must tell it to add 1. We do this by typing: 30 N = N + 1
This tells the computer that the new value of N is obtained by adding 1 to the old value of N.

Now we want the computer to print the new value of N. Instead of saying PRINT N again, we take advantage of the fact that we gave this instruction in an earlier step. We type: 40 GOTO 20
This tells the computer, when it runs the program, that after step 40 it goes to step 20, and then goes on to step 30, etc.

After you have stored this program, to get it to run, type RUN and press the ENTER key. You will see immediately that we are in trouble. The number ladder has no top. The computer is printing the numbers as we asked it to, but it will go on forever. We forgot to tell it when to stop.

To get it to stop now, press the BREAK key. To get the program on the screen, type LIST and press the ENTER key. We have to insert another step to tell the computer when to stop. Type:

35 IF N = 21 THEN STOP

Press the ENTER key. The computer will put this step between step 30 and step 40. This step requires the computer to make a decision. It must compare the number that N stands for with the number 21. If they are not the same, it skips the STOP instruction and then keeps going. If they are the same, it will stop. Step 35 allows it to print only the numbers from 1 to 20.

A convenient way of showing what the computer has to do in this program is to draw a flowchart. In a flowchart, each step that *must* be carried out is put into a box. A step that requires a decision about what to do next is put into a diamond. The program has two branches going out of the diamond, showing the two possible decisions. The decision that says GOTO 20 is shown by the arrow that goes back to the PRINT N instruction.

The return from a later step to an earlier one forms what is called a *loop*. A program with a loop will run forever unless a step is provided for breaking out of the loop, like our step 35.

Here is the program for printing the natural numbers from 1 to 20:

```
10 N = 1
20 PRINT N
30 N = N + 1
35 IF N = 21 THEN STOP
40 GOTO 20
```

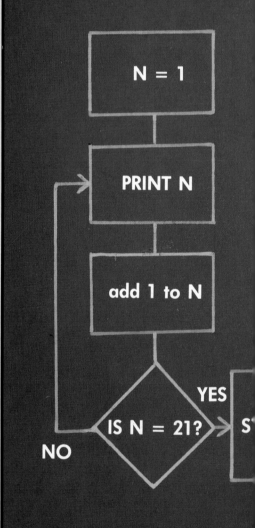

1+1=

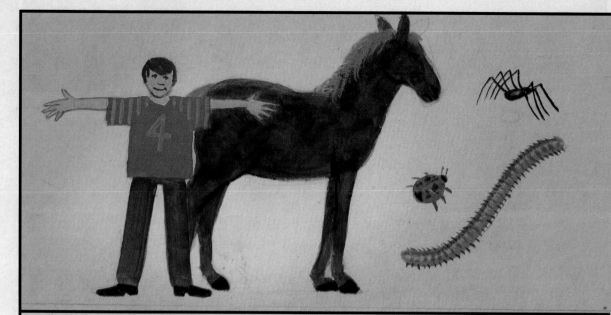

Evens and Odds

Some things come in pairs. For example, the legs of a person, a horse, an insect, and a centipede come in pairs. When things come in pairs, their number is called an *even* number. The first even number is 2. To get the rest, climb up the number ladder from rung 2 by going up two rungs at a time. The list of even numbers begins with 2, 4, 6, 8, 10, and goes on without ending. All the other natural numbers are called *odd* numbers. The first odd number is 1. To get the rest, climb up the number ladder from rung 1 and skip all the even numbers. To do this you have to go up two rungs at a time.

It is useful to picture a number as the number of checkers on a table. Then the various ways in which the checkers can be arranged give us some information about the number. For example, this procedure can show us how even numbers differ from odd numbers. An even number of checkers can always be arranged in two lines with the same number of checkers in each line. An odd number of checkers cannot. No matter how you arrange an odd number of checkers in two lines, one line always has more checkers than the other.

If you take any odd number of checkers greater than 1, you can arrange them in an L with the same number of checkers in each leg of the L. For example, the L formed with three checkers has two

22

20

18

16

14

12

10

8

6

4

2

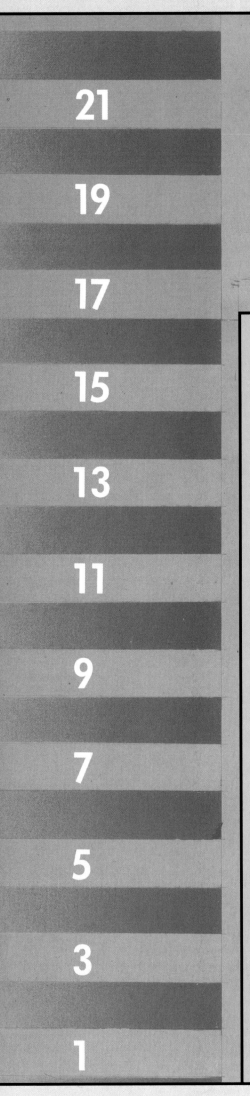

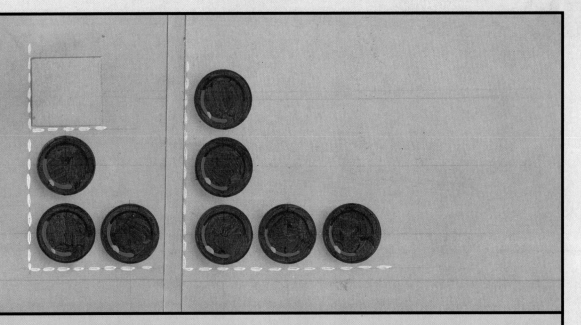

checkers in each leg; one with five checkers has three checkers in each leg. Notice that the checker at the corner of the L belongs to both legs. Even though a single checker picturing the number 1 doesn't look like an L, we can think of it as an L with shrunken legs. An even number of checkers cannot be arranged to form an L with the same number of checkers in each leg of the L.

We can get a hand calculator to display the odd numbers, one after the other, by slightly changing the method we used to get it to display the natural numbers. Start with 1, and instead of adding 1 at each step, add 2 at each step. Here is the sequence of keystrokes for doing this: 1 + 2 =
To display the even numbers one after the other, start with 2 and add 2 at each step. The sequence of keystrokes looks like this: 2 + 2 =

To instruct a computer to print the odd numbers from 1 to 45, we must tell it to stop when it reaches 47. How would you change the flowchart for printing the natural numbers from 1 to 21 to turn it into a flowchart for printing the odd numbers from 1 to 45? (See answer 1, printed upside down.)

How would you change the basic program on pages 8–11 to turn it into a program for printing the odd numbers from 1 to 45? (See answer 2.)

How would you change the flowchart for printing the natural numbers from 1 to 21 to turn it into a flowchart for printing the even numbers from 2 to 40? (See answer 3.)

How would you change the basic program on pages 8–11 to turn it into a program for printing the even numbers from 2 to 40? (See answer 4.)

Answers:
1. In the third box from the top write: Add 2 to N. In the diamond write: Is N=47?.
2. Change step 30 to say: N=N+2. Change step 35 to say: IF N=47 THEN STOP.
3. In the first box write: N=2. In the third box write: Add 2 to N. In the diamond write: Is N=42?.
4. Change step 10 to say: N=2. Change step 30 to say: N=N+2. Change step 35 to say: IF N=42 THEN STOP.

Written Numbers

The symbols we use for writing numbers are called *numerals*. There are many different ways of writing numbers. The simplest and oldest way is to cut notches in a stick or draw lines on a sheet of paper. Three lines stand for the number *three*. We still use this system when we write the Roman numerals I, II, and III. We find it hidden, too, in our Arabic numerals 2 and 3. They began as sets of separated strokes. Then when the strokes were written in a hurry, they were joined to each other.

The old system is not good for writing large numbers: To write the number *one million* in this system, you would have to write a million strokes on paper! To overcome this difficulty, people began to use special symbols for some numbers greater than one, and combined them to write the other numbers. The Romans, for example, used V for five, X for ten, and L for fifty. Then they wrote IV for one less than five, and VI for one more than five. But this system also has a disadvantage. To write larger and larger numbers you would need more and more new symbols. The Hindus solved this problem by using a system that needs only ten symbols, the digits 0, 1, 2, 3, 4, 5, 6, 7, 8, 9. Arabic numerals are based on this Hindu discovery: With these ten digits you can write down any number you like, because in this system, the number that a digit stands for depends on where it is written. The digit 2 written in the first column on the right stands for two *ones*. The same digit written in the second column from the right stands for two *tens*. Written in the third column from the right, it stands for two *hundreds* (ten times ten). To make this system work we use the symbol 0 to stand for "none." Thus 20 means 2 tens plus no ones. This type of system is called a *place-value* system.

Underlying a place-value system is the idea of a *base*. The base is the number of separate symbols the system uses. The value of 1 in the second column from the right is the base. In the third column it is base times base. In the fourth column it is base times base times base, and so on. In Arabic numerals the base is ten.

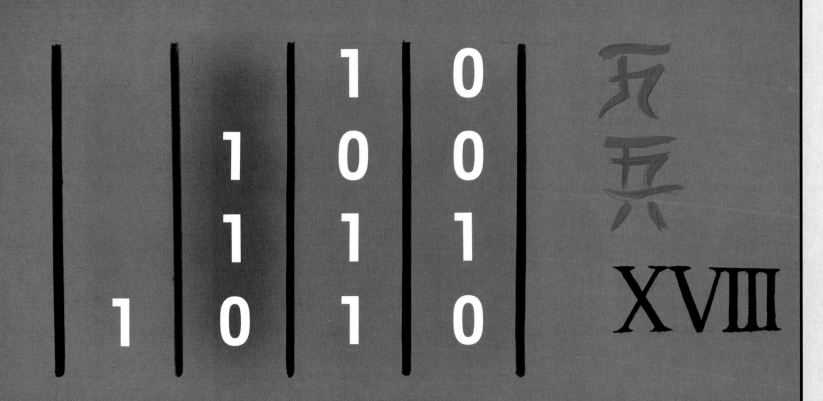

There are other place-value systems that use a different base. A very important one used by computers is the *binary* system that uses only the symbols 0 and 1, called "bits." In this system a 1 in the first column on the right stands for one. In the second column it stands for two. In the third column it stands for two times two, or four. Every time you move it one place to the left you double its value. Thus, in the binary system, 10 means 1 two plus no ones. 100 means 1 four plus no twos plus no ones. 111 means 1 four plus 1 two plus 1 one, or seven. The binary system has the simplest and shortest addition and multiplication tables that are possible. Here they are:

Binary Addition	Binary Multiplication
$0 + 0 = 0$	$0 \times 0 = 0$
$0 + 1 = 1$	$0 \times 1 = 0$
$1 + 0 = 1$	$1 \times 0 = 0$
$1 + 1 = 10$	$1 \times 1 = 1$

Computers also use the "hexadecimal" system in which the base is sixteen. The sixteen symbols it uses are 0, 1, 2, 3, 4, 5, 6, 7, 8, 9 for the numbers zero to nine, and A, B, C, D, E, F for the numbers ten to fifteen. In this system, a 1 in the second column from the right stands for sixteen. In the third column it stands for sixteen times sixteen, or two hundred fifty-six. Thus, in the hexadecimal system, 21 stands for 2 sixteens plus 1 one, or thirty-three. 3B stands for 3 sixteens plus eleven ones, or fifty-nine. What does 4C stand for in this system?

Answer: seventy-six.

15

Rewards and Penalties

There are some games in which a player may receive either a reward or a penalty. For example, suppose the game is tossing a coin and guessing whether it comes up heads or tails. If you guess right, you have a reward of one point. If you guess wrong, you have a penalty of one point. A natural number can be used to show how many reward points the player has earned. A new kind of number is needed to show how many penalty points were earned. We call these new numbers *negative* numbers. They are written with a minus sign on the left: -1 is called "negative one"; -2 is called "negative two"; and so on. In situations where negative numbers may be used, the natural numbers are called "positive" numbers. Zero is neither negative nor positive.

Negative numbers have many uses. In business, they can be used to show a loss, while a positive number shows a gain. On a thermometer, positive numbers show temperatures above zero, and negative numbers show temperatures below zero.

The main fact about a penalty of one point is that it wipes out a reward of one point. This fact suggests an easy way of adding numbers, some of which may be negative. Put black checkers on a table to picture a positive number (one checker for each point); and put red checkers on the table to picture a negative number. Form as many pairs as you can with one black checker and one red checker in each pair. Since a penalty wipes out a reward, each such pair represents zero and is removed from the table. Then checkers of only one color remain, and they represent the sum. For example, to add -7 and 4, put seven red checkers and four black checkers on the table. Four pairs can be formed, each with one red and one black checker. Remove these pairs from the table. Then there are 3 red checkers left. Since they represent -3, we know that $(-7) + (4) = -3$.

Use checkers to find the following sums: $(-5) + (-3)$; $(-8) + (2)$; $(9) + (-4)$.

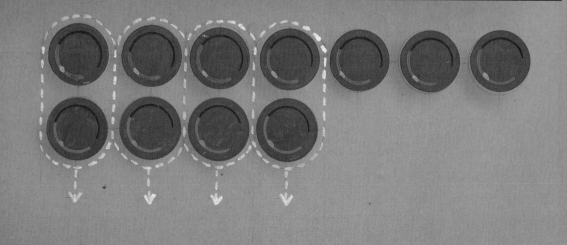

The Straight Line

Many different paths may be used to go from one point to another. The shortest possible path is the one that is straight. How can we make a straight line? One way is to draw one with a ruler. But that way we use one straight line (the edge of the ruler) to make another. How can we make a straight line without using a ruler? One way is to pull on the ends of a string until it is taut. Another is to hold one end of a string while the other end is pulled down by a weight that is tied to it. The string with a weight is called a "plumb line" and is used to make a *vertical* line, one that points to the center of the earth. A bricklayer uses both methods.

You can also make a straight line with a piece of paper. Simply fold it and press the crease flat. Then the crease is a straight line.

Directions and Angles

If two people stand back to back, they face in *opposite* directions. In the drawing below, an arrow shows the direction in which each person is facing. Arrows can always be used to picture directions.

The drawing to the right shows a bug standing on a straight line. If the bug moves by crawling along the line, there are only two directions in which it might move. The arrows on the line drawn from the position of the bug show these two directions. There are two opposite directions on any straight line. We give names to some special directions, but the same name doesn't always mean the same direction. The two opposite directions on the line that joins your shoulders are called *left* and *right*. Left is from your head to your left arm, and right is from your head to your right arm. If two people stand back to back, what is right for one is left for the other. On the surface of the earth *down* is toward the center of the earth and *up* points away from the center.

The earth spins on its axis, like a top. The points on the surface of the earth that are on the axis are called the *north pole* and the *south pole*. There are many circles on the earth that join the north pole and south pole. They are called *meridians*. Every point on the surface of the earth that is not at one of the poles has only one meridian through it. Because the meridian circle is so large, a small piece of it is almost straight. At a point that is not a pole, the direction on this (almost) straight piece that points to the north pole is called "north" and the opposite direction is called "south." At the north pole all directions are south, and at the south pole all directions are north.

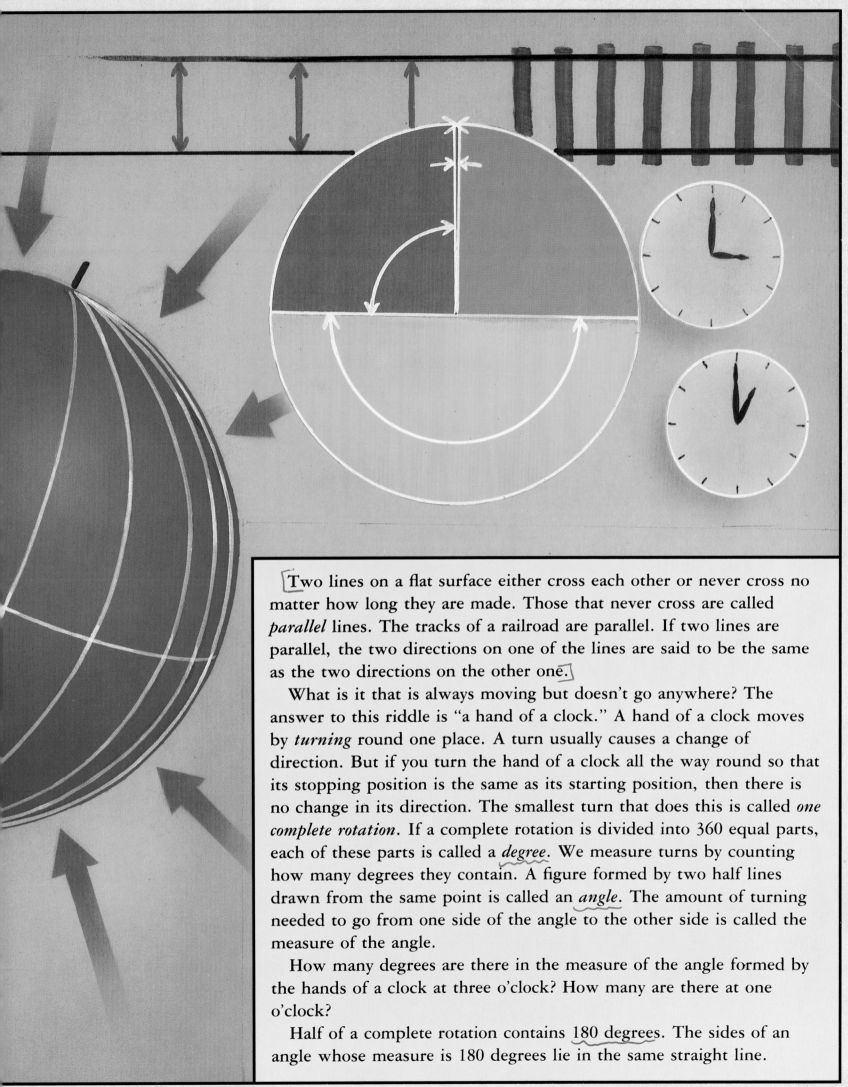

Two lines on a flat surface either cross each other or never cross no matter how long they are made. Those that never cross are called *parallel* lines. The tracks of a railroad are parallel. If two lines are parallel, the two directions on one of the lines are said to be the same as the two directions on the other one.

What is it that is always moving but doesn't go anywhere? The answer to this riddle is "a hand of a clock." A hand of a clock moves by *turning* round one place. A turn usually causes a change of direction. But if you turn the hand of a clock all the way round so that its stopping position is the same as its starting position, then there is no change in its direction. The smallest turn that does this is called *one complete rotation*. If a complete rotation is divided into 360 equal parts, each of these parts is called a *degree*. We measure turns by counting how many degrees they contain. A figure formed by two half lines drawn from the same point is called an *angle*. The amount of turning needed to go from one side of the angle to the other side is called the measure of the angle.

How many degrees are there in the measure of the angle formed by the hands of a clock at three o'clock? How many are there at one o'clock?

Half of a complete rotation contains 180 degrees. The sides of an angle whose measure is 180 degrees lie in the same straight line.

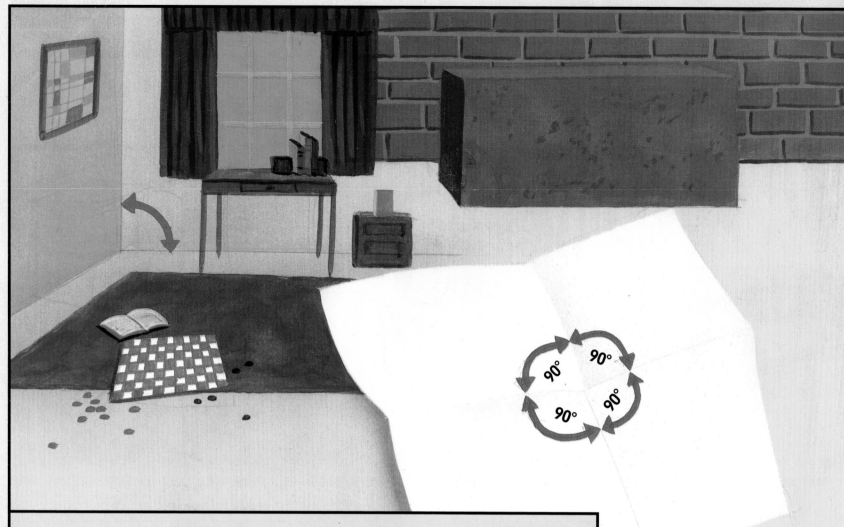

Right Angles

An angle whose measure is 90 degrees is called a *right angle*. It is one quarter of a complete rotation. In each corner of your room, you probably have three right angles, one in the floor, and two in the walls that meet at that corner.

You can make a right angle without the help of any measuring instrument by folding paper. Fold a sheet of paper and press the crease flat. As we saw on page 17 the crease is a straight line. Now fold the paper again so that the two parts of the crease come together. This makes a second crease. Press this crease flat. When you unfold the paper, you will see four right angles at the point where the two creases meet. They completely fill the space around that point.

A four-sided figure whose sides meet at right angles is called a *rectangle*. The six faces of a brick are all rectangles. That is why bricks are useful for building walls. Two right angles added form an angle whose sides are in the same straight line. So bricks stacked side by side or on top of each other can form straight lines.

A *square* is a rectangle whose sides all have the same length. To make a square without a ruler, fold a rectangular sheet of paper putting a short edge onto a long edge. Cut away the single layer that extends beyond the double layer. The double layer, unfolded, will be a square.

Rectangular Numbers

A ny number of checkers can be arranged in a line. But only some numbers of checkers can be arranged in two or more equal rows placed one under the other to form a rectangle with more than one checker in each row. For example, six checkers can form a rectangle with two rows and three checkers in each row. They can also form a rectangle with three rows and two checkers in each row. Twelve checkers can form a rectangle with two rows and six checkers in each row; a rectangle with three rows and four checkers in each row; a rectangle with four rows and three checkers in each row; and one with six rows and two checkers in each row. Numbers that can form rectangles with more than one row and more than one checker in each row are called *composite* numbers.

Whenever checkers form a rectangle, the number of checkers in the rectangle is equal to the number of rows times the number of checkers in each row. For this reason, a rectangular array of checkers is like a picture of multiplication.

Form a picture of 5×7 by arranging checkers in 5 rows with 7 checkers in each row. If we imagine the rectangle turned to make its left side its top side, then we see it is also an arrangement in 7 rows with 5 checkers in each row. This shows that $5 \times 7 = 7 \times 5$. Whenever two numbers are multiplied, the two numbers can change places without changing the product. This fact is very useful. It means that, instead of memorizing the whole multiplication table, it is good enough to memorize only half of it. If you know that 7×9 equals 63, then you know at once that 9×7 also equals 63.

2 x 3

x 2

2 x 6

x 2

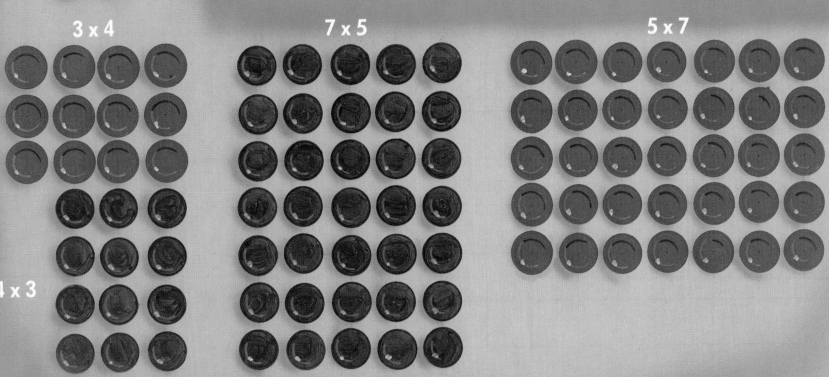

3 x 4

7 x 5

5 x 7

4 x 3

Prime Numbers

There are some numbers of checkers that cannot form a rectangle with more than one row and more than one checker in each row. They can only form a single line of checkers. Such numbers are called *prime numbers*. 2, 3, and 5 are prime numbers. What is the next higher prime number?

The Greek scientist Eratosthenes, who lived over two thousand years ago, invented a method for identifying the prime numbers in their natural order, one after another. His method is called the *sieve of Eratosthenes*. Here it is: Write the natural numbers in a line, starting with 2. On the next line write the numbers from this line that remain when you leave out 2 and all the numbers you can get when you count by twos (the multiples of 2). The first number in this line will be 3. On the next line write the numbers from that line that remain when you leave out 3 and all multiples of 3. The first number in this line will be 5. On the next line write the numbers from that line that remain when you leave out 5 and all multiples of 5. The first number in this line will be 7. Continue in this way, writing under each line the numbers from that line that remain when you leave out the first number in the line and all its multiples. The prime numbers are the numbers that are first in all these lines.

Every composite number can be written as a product of prime numbers. For example, $12 = 2 \times 2 \times 3$; $15 = 3 \times 5$; $28 = 2 \times 2 \times 7$.

Write 72 as a product of prime numbers.

2	3	4	5	6	7	8	9	10	11	12	13
	3		5		7		9		11		
			5		7				11		
					7				11		
									11		

1	6		1	9
2	3		3	3
3	2		9	1
6	1			

Divisors

When you divide 2 into 6, the quotient is 3 and there is no remainder. When you divide 2 into 7, the quotient is 3, and the remainder is 1. We call one number a *divisor* of another if it can divide into it without a remainder. So 2 is a divisor of 6, but it is not a divisor of 7. To find all the divisors of a number, take that number of checkers and arrange them in all possible ways either in a line or in rectangles with more than one row and more than one checker in each row. Each arrangement shows you two divisors of the number: One is the number of rows, and the other is the number of checkers in each row. For example, with 6 checkers you can form 1 row with 6 checkers in the row, 2 rows with 3 checkers in each row, 3 rows with 2 checkers in each row, and 6 rows with 1 checker in each row. So we know that the divisors of 6 are 1, 2, 3, and 6. With 7 checkers you can form 1 row with 7 checkers in the row, and 7 rows with 1 checker in each row, but you cannot form any rectangles with more than one row and more than one checker in each row. So the only divisors of 7 are 1 and 7. *The only divisors of a prime number are 1 and the number itself.*

Arrange the pairs of divisors of a number in a table with two columns, one column for the number of rows, and the other column for the number of checkers in each row. Start with one row and increase the number of rows gradually. You will see that the two columns contain the same numbers. In one column, the divisors increase gradually from the smallest divisor, which is 1. In the other column, they decrease gradually from the largest divisor, which is the number itself. To get the complete list of divisors without repeating them, we need only the upper half of the table. For some numbers, like 9, it is possible to form a rectangle in which the number of rows is equal to the number of checkers in each row. For such a number, to get all its divisors, end the table with the line where the number of rows equals the number of checkers in each row.

A divisor of a number that is less than the number itself is called a *proper divisor*. Since the only divisors of a prime number are 1 and the number itself, every prime number has only one proper divisor, the number 1.

Square Numbers

A number of checkers that can form a square, where the number of rows equals the number of checkers in each row, is called a *square number*. You get a square number whenever you multiply some number by itself. Since $1 \times 1 = 1$, $2 \times 2 = 4$, $3 \times 3 = 9$, $4 \times 4 = 16$, and $5 \times 5 = 25$, the first five square numbers are 1, 4, 9, 16, and 25.

There is an interesting connection between the odd numbers and the square numbers: Start with 1 and then add the next odd number (3) to it. Then add to the sum one more odd number at a time, taking the odd numbers in their proper order. The sums will give the square numbers in their proper order. This is shown in the table below:

$$1 = 1$$
$$1 + 3 = 4$$
$$1 + 3 + 5 = 9$$
$$1 + 3 + 5 + 7 = 16$$
$$1 + 3 + 5 + 7 + 9 = 25$$

We can write a computer program that will do the addition for us, and stop at any place that we choose. We do this by making some small changes in the computer program we already have for printing the odd numbers. We used the letter N for the odd numbers the program produces. Let us use the letter S to stand for the sum we get each time we add another odd number. The first value of S is 1. Remember that we produce a new value of N by adding 2 to the old value. We tell this to the computer by saying $N = N + 2$. Now we want to produce a new value of S by adding the new value of N to the old value of S. So immediately after we get the new value of N, we tell the computer $S = S + N$. We also tell the computer when to stop. Suppose we ask it to stop when $N = 41$.

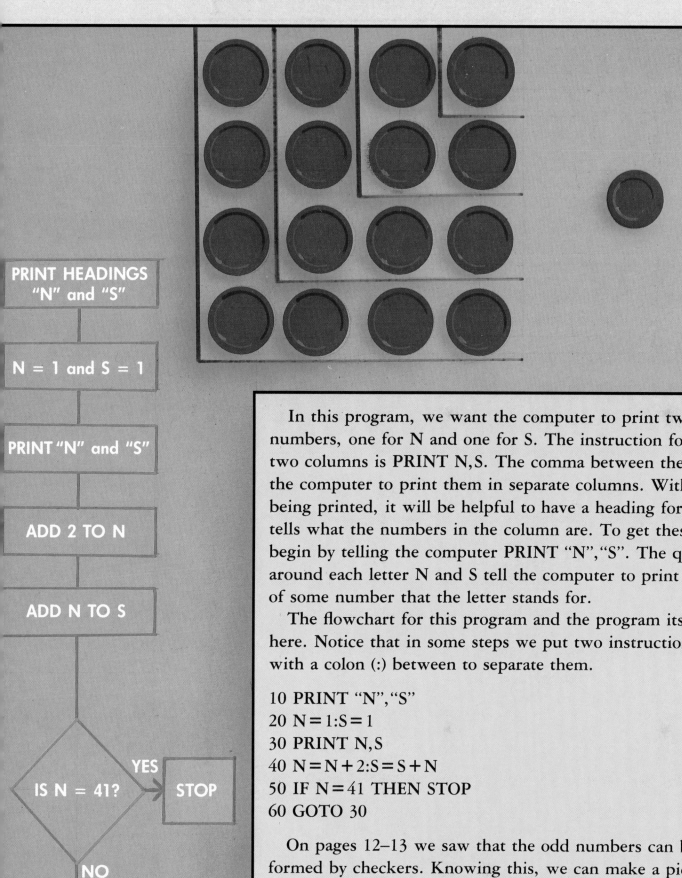

PRINT HEADINGS
"N" and "S"

N = 1 and S = 1

PRINT "N" and "S"

ADD 2 TO N

ADD N TO S

IS N = 41? → YES → STOP

NO

In this program, we want the computer to print two columns of numbers, one for N and one for S. The instruction for printing these two columns is PRINT N,S. The comma between the N and the S tells the computer to print them in separate columns. With two columns being printed, it will be helpful to have a heading for each column that tells what the numbers in the column are. To get these headings, we begin by telling the computer PRINT "N","S". The quotation marks around each letter N and S tell the computer to print the letter instead of some number that the letter stands for.

The flowchart for this program and the program itself are shown here. Notice that in some steps we put two instructions into one step with a colon (:) between to separate them.

```
10 PRINT "N","S"
20 N = 1:S = 1
30 PRINT N,S
40 N = N + 2:S = S + N
50 IF N = 41 THEN STOP
60 GOTO 30
```

On pages 12–13 we saw that the odd numbers can be pictured as L's formed by checkers. Knowing this, we can make a picture that explains why adding the odd numbers starting with 1 produces the square numbers. Put a single checker on a table. It represents both the odd number 1 and the square number 1. Now put next to it the L that pictures the odd number 3. Place it so that the single checker is inside the angle of the L. This produces a 2 by 2 square with 4 checkers in it. Now put down the next larger L that pictures the odd number 5. Place it so that the square made before is inside the angle of the L. Continue in this way, adding larger and larger L's as shown in the drawing. Every time another L is added, the next larger square is formed.

Triangles

If you nail three straight wooden bars end to end, you make a triangle. If you nail four bars, you form a quadrilateral. By grasping two opposite corners of the quadrilateral and pushing, you can make them move toward each other. If you pull, you can make them move away from each other. Either way you can make the quadrilateral change its shape. A triangle behaves differently. If you grasp any two of its corners and push or pull, the corners will not move closer to each other or apart, and the shape of the triangle will not change. The triangle is *rigid* while the quadrilateral is not. This explains why trusses are used in bridges to make a series of triangles. Because the triangles are rigid, they prevent the bridge from collapsing under its usual load.

Cut a triangle out of paper and label its three corners A, B, and C. There is an angle at each corner. Hold the triangle so that the side BC is at the bottom and the angle A is at the top. Fold the top down to put point A on the line BC in such a way that the crease is parallel to BC. Now make two more folds to bring the angle at B and the angle at C next to the angle at A. Then you can see that the measures of the three angles add up to 180 degrees, since the angle formed by adding them has its sides in the same straight line. This is something all triangles have in common.

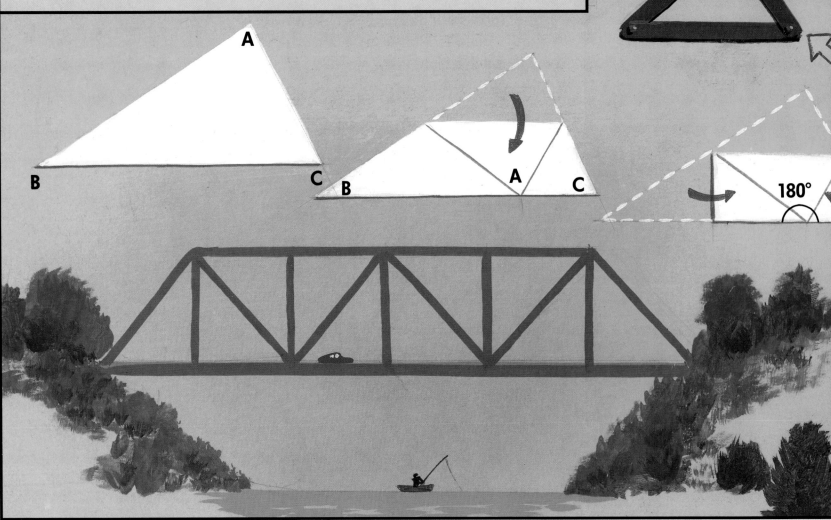

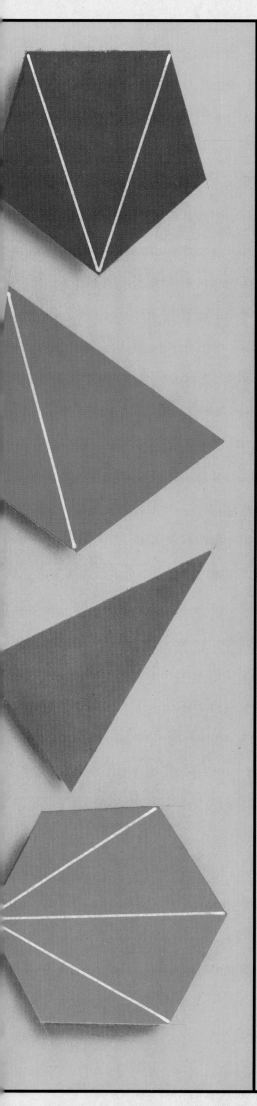

Polygons

A closed figure with straight sides is called a *polygon*. A triangle is a polygon with three sides. A quadrilateral is a polygon with four sides. A polygon with five sides is called a *pentagon*. One with six sides is called a *hexagon*.

A line joining two corners of a polygon that are not on the same side is called a *diagonal*. In any polygon, choose one corner, and then draw as many diagonals as you can from that corner. The diagonals divide the polygon into triangles. In the quadrilateral, which has four sides, there are two such triangles. In the pentagon, which has five sides, there are three such triangles. In the hexagon, which has six sides, there are four such triangles. When you divide any polygon into triangles by drawing all the diagonals you can from one corner, the number of triangles is always *two less* than the number of sides of the polygon.

Now look at the angles of the polygon. Two of them have no diagonal through them. The others are each cut into parts by the diagonals, and each part is an angle of one of the triangles. Adding the measures of the angles of the polygon is like adding the measures of the angles of all the triangles.

A quadrilateral is divided into two triangles, and each triangle contributes 180 degrees to the sum of the angles, so the angles of the quadrilateral add up to 2 × 180 degrees, or 360 degrees. A pentagon is divided into three triangles, so the angles of a pentagon add up to 3 × 180 degrees, or 540 degrees. The angles of a hexagon add up to 4 × 180 degrees, or 720 degrees. The angles of a polygon always add up to 180 degrees times two less than the number of sides of the polygon.

Here is a computer program that uses this rule to calculate the sum of the measures of the angles of a polygon. In this program N stands for the number of sides of the polygon, and S stands for the sum of the angles. This program uses a new method for telling the computer what values of N to use.

Step 20 tells the computer the first and last values of N to use. After the results of a calculation are printed in step 40, step 50 tells the computer to change the value of N by adding 1 and then to go to step 30. When the last value of N is reached, the computer stops.

Notice the star in step 30. It is the symbol used in computer language to mean "times."

```
10 PRINT "N","S"
20 FOR N=3 TO 25
30 S=(N−2)*180
40 PRINT N,S
50 NEXT N
```

Triangular Numbers

Put one checker on a table. Under it put two checkers. Under the two checkers, put three checkers, and so on. Each time you add a line of checkers, use one more checker than you had in the line before, as shown in the drawing. As you proceed, the checkers form larger and larger triangles. The number of checkers in each triangle is called a *triangular number*. The first triangular number is 1. The second one is $1+2$. The third one is $1+2+3$. The fourth one is $1+2+3+4$, and so on. When you add all the natural numbers from 1 up to any given number, the sum is a triangular number.

The fiftieth triangular number is the sum of all the numbers from 1 to 50. Writing down the fifty numbers and then adding them is a big job. Fortunately there is a shortcut for getting the sum. To discover this shortcut, make a triangle of any size that pictures a triangular number. Then make another one of the same size, but upside down. Notice first that the number of lines of checkers put down to make the triangle is the same as the number of checkers in the last line. Now put the two triangles together as shown in the drawing to form a rectangle. The number of rows of checkers in the rectangle is the same as the number of checkers in the last line of each triangle. The number of checkers in each row of the rectangle is one more than that number. We know that to find the number of checkers in a rectangle you multiply the number of rows by the number of checkers in each row. Half of that product will be the triangular number we are looking for, since each triangle is half of the rectangle. So, to find the fiftieth triangular number take half of 50 × 51. The answer is 1275.

You can also write a computer program for printing out triangular numbers one after another. Simply make two changes in the program for adding the odd numbers that appears on page 13: In step 40, instead of saying $N = N + 2$, say $N = N + 1$. Then the computer will climb the number ladder one step at a time instead of two steps at a time, and so will produce all the natural numbers instead of only the odd numbers. In step 50, choose any number at which you want the computer to stop.

Triangular numbers have another interesting quality that is fun to discover. Make a triangle that pictures a triangular number. Then put next to it upside down the next larger triangle, as shown in the drawing. Together they form a square. So the sum of two consecutive triangular numbers is always a square number. Here is a list of the first fifteen triangular numbers: 1, 3, 6, 10, 15, 21, 28, 36, 45, 55, 66, 78, 91, 105, 120. If you add any two that are next to each other in this list, you get a square number: $1 + 3 = 4$, $3 + 6 = 9$, $6 + 10 = 16$, and so on.

Square Root

You get a square number when you multiply a natural number by itself. If N stands for a number, we use the symbol N^2 to stand for N times N, and read it as "N square." The first table at the right shows values of N from 1 to 4 in the first column. The second column shows their squares. The second table is the same table written backward. The second column in that table tells you what number you must multiply by itself to get the number in the first column. The number in the second column is called the *square root* of the number in the first column.

The second table shows that the square root of 1 is 1, because $1 \times 1 = 1$. It shows that the square root of 4 is 2, because $2 \times 2 = 4$. The square root of 9 is 3 because $3 \times 3 = 9$, and so on. Notice that there are numbers missing in the first column of the second table: The numbers 2 and 3, which are between 1 and 4, are missing. The numbers 5, 6, 7, and 8, which are between 4 and 9, are missing, and so on. These numbers also have square roots. They are missing from the table because their square roots are not natural numbers. But they do have square roots, and we shall now find a way of calculating them.

First we must know how to recognize a square root. We already

Table of
Square Roots

1	1
4	2
9	3
16	4

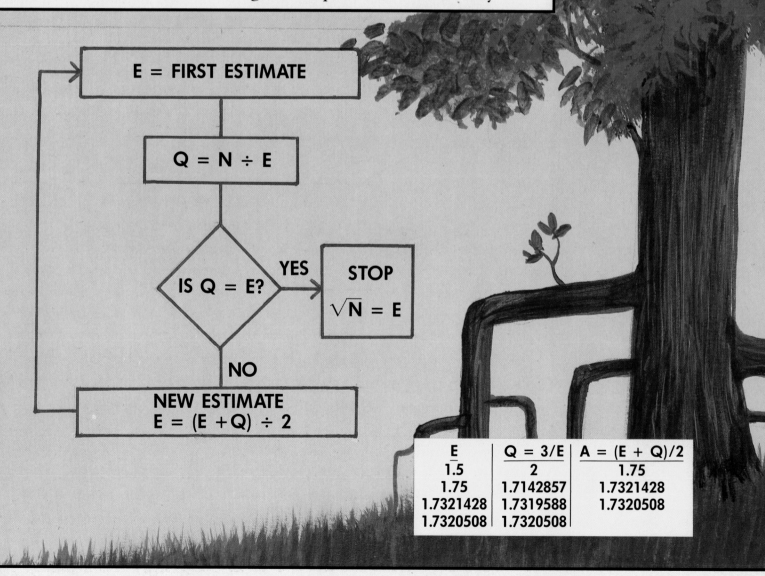

E = FIRST ESTIMATE

Q = N ÷ E

IS Q = E? —YES→ STOP √N = E

NO

NEW ESTIMATE
E = (E + Q) ÷ 2

E	Q = 3/E	A = (E + Q)/2
1.5	2	1.75
1.75	1.7142857	1.7321428
1.7321428	1.7319588	1.7320508
1.7320508	1.7320508	

know that 2 is the square root of 4 because $2 \times 2 = 4$. This also means that if 2 is divided into 4, the quotient is 2. 3 is the square root of 9 because $3 \times 3 = 9$. This also means that if 3 is divided into 9, the quotient is 3. Here is our clue: If you divide one number into another and the quotient is equal to the divisor, then that divisor is the square root of the number you divided into.

Some calculators have a square root key with the symbol $\sqrt{}$ on it. With such a calculator, you key in a number and then press the square root key. The calculator then displays the square root of that number. However, it is possible to find the square root of a number using a calculator that does not have a square root key.

The method we use is to creep up on the answer by first making a guess or estimate and then step by step making better and better estimates. The flowchart shows the procedure. N stands for the number whose square root we are looking for. E is the first estimate. Divide N by E and call the quotient Q. Then see whether or not $Q = E$. If it is, then E is the square root we are looking for.

If Q does not equal E, then one of the two numbers E or Q is too small to be the square root, and the other one is too large. This means that the square root is some number that is between E and Q. So we take as our next improved estimate the average of E and Q, which is halfway between them. The average is calculated by adding E and Q and then dividing by 2. We let this average be the new value of E and we go back to the division step. We repeat this procedure over and over again until E and Q are the same or almost the same.

As an example, we shall find the square root of 3. We first prepare a table with three columns, labeled E, $Q = 3/E$, and $A = (E + Q)/2$. In these labels the symbol "/" is the computer symbol for "divided by," and A stands for the average of E and Q.

Since 3 is between 1 and 4, whose square roots are 1 and 2 respectively, the square root of 3 must be between 1 and 2. Let's use as our first guess $E = 1.5$. This is the first entry in the first column.

Now use the calculator to divide 3 by 1.5 by pressing keys in this order: $3 \div 1.5 =$. The calculator then displays the value of Q. Write this in the second column. Now press the keys $+ 1.5 = \div 2 =$. The calculator will then display the value of A. Write this in the third column. This will be your new estimate, so you also write it on the next line in the first column.

Now, using the new value of E, divide 3 by E. Write the answer in the second column. Add E to this answer and then divide by 2. Write the result in the third column and in the first column of the next line.

Do this over and over again until you get values of E and Q that are almost the same or until the values of E begin to repeat. The table shows that a very good estimate for the square root of 3 is 1.7320508.

Use the same procedure to find the square root of 10. When you do, the heading for the second column should be $Q = 10/E$.

Perfect, Amicable, and Sociable Numbers

A natural number is called *perfect* if it is equal to the sum of all its proper divisors. For example, the proper divisors of 6 are 1, 2, and 3. Since $1+2+3=6$, 6 is a perfect number. The proper divisors of 28 are 1, 2, 4, 7, and 14. Since $1+2+4+7+14=28$, 28 is a perfect number. The next higher perfect number is 496.

Two numbers are called *amicable* (friendly) if the sum of the proper divisors of each is equal to the other. For example, the proper divisors of 220 are 1, 2, 4, 5, 10, 11, 20, 22, 44, 55, and 110, and they add up to 284. The proper divisors of 284 are 1, 2, 4, 71, and 142, and they add up to 220. So 220 and 284 are amicable numbers.

A series of numbers is called a *sociable chain* if, when you arrange them in a circle, the sum of the proper divisors of each one of them is equal to the next number in the circle (always in the same direction around the circle). The drawings show two sociable chains, one with five numbers in the chain, and one with twenty-eight numbers in the chain.

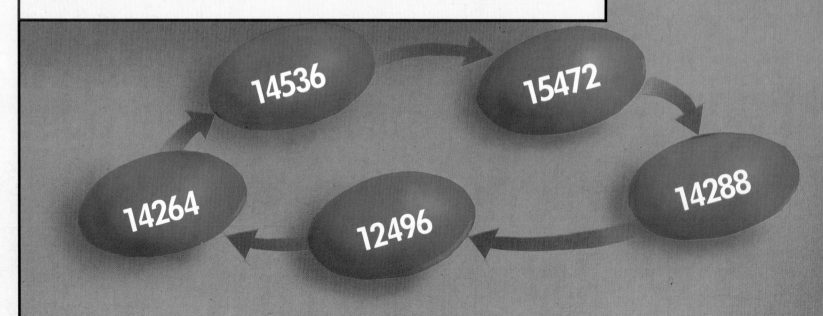

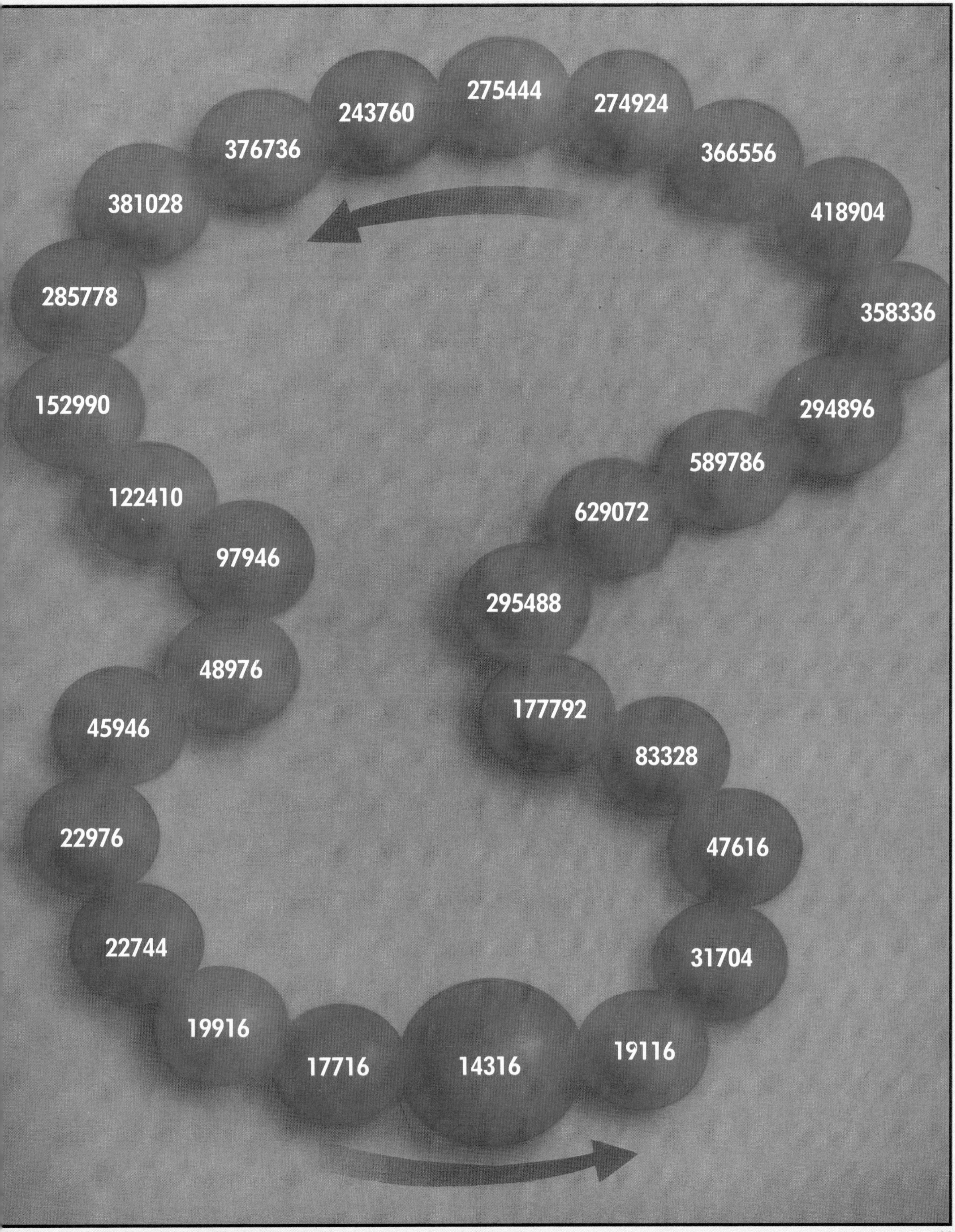
14316
19116
31704
47616
83328
177792
295488
629072
589786
294896
358336
418904
366556
274924
275444
243760
376736
381028
285778
152990
122410
97946
48976
45946
22976
22744
19916
17716

A Multipurpose Program

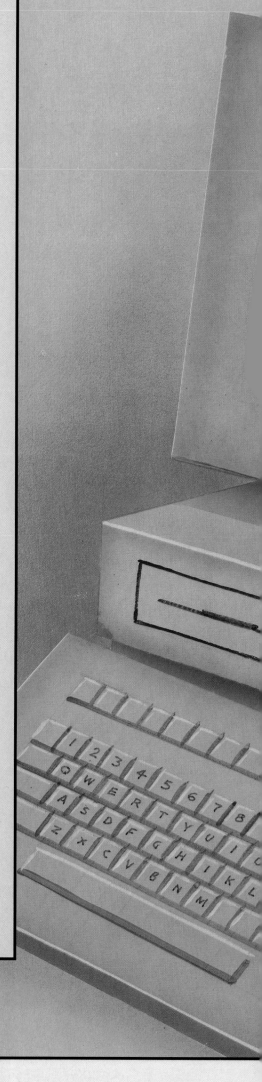

Here is a computer program for finding the sum of the proper divisors of any number greater than 4. It can be used to identify perfect numbers, prime numbers, amicable numbers, and sociable chains.

```
20 S=1
30 INPUT A
35 IF A<5 THEN GOTO 210
40 B=SQR(A)
50 C=INT(B)
60 IF B=C THEN S=S+C
70 IF B=C THEN M=C−1
80 IF B>C THEN M=C
90 D=2
100 Q=A/D
110 E=INT(Q)
120 IF Q=E THEN S=S+D+Q
130 IF D<M THEN GOTO 200
140 LPRINT "A=";A, "S=";S:STOP
150 A=S:S=1:GOTO 35
200 D=D+1:GOTO 100
210 PRINT "Program not good for A<5.":STOP
```

In step 20, because 1 is a proper divisor of every number greater than 1, we use it as the first value of S, the sum of the proper divisors of A. As we identify more proper divisors, steps 60 and 120 add them to S.

At step 30 the program stops running while it waits for you to key in the number A. Then you press the ENTER key to tell the computer to go on with the calculation.

Step 40 finds the square root of A, and step 50 drops the fractional part of the square root to get a whole number C. If C itself is the square root of A, it is a proper divisor of A, and step 60 adds it to S.

The program tests a series of numbers D to see if they are divisors of A. The first value of D, given in step 90, is 2. Step 100 finds the quotient Q=A/D. Step 110 drops the fractional part of the quotient to get a whole number. If the quotient is that whole number, then D is a divisor of A. In that case step 120 adds both D and Q to S, since then both D and Q are divisors of A. Step 200 adds 1 to D to get a new trial divisor, and steps 100 and 120 are repeated.

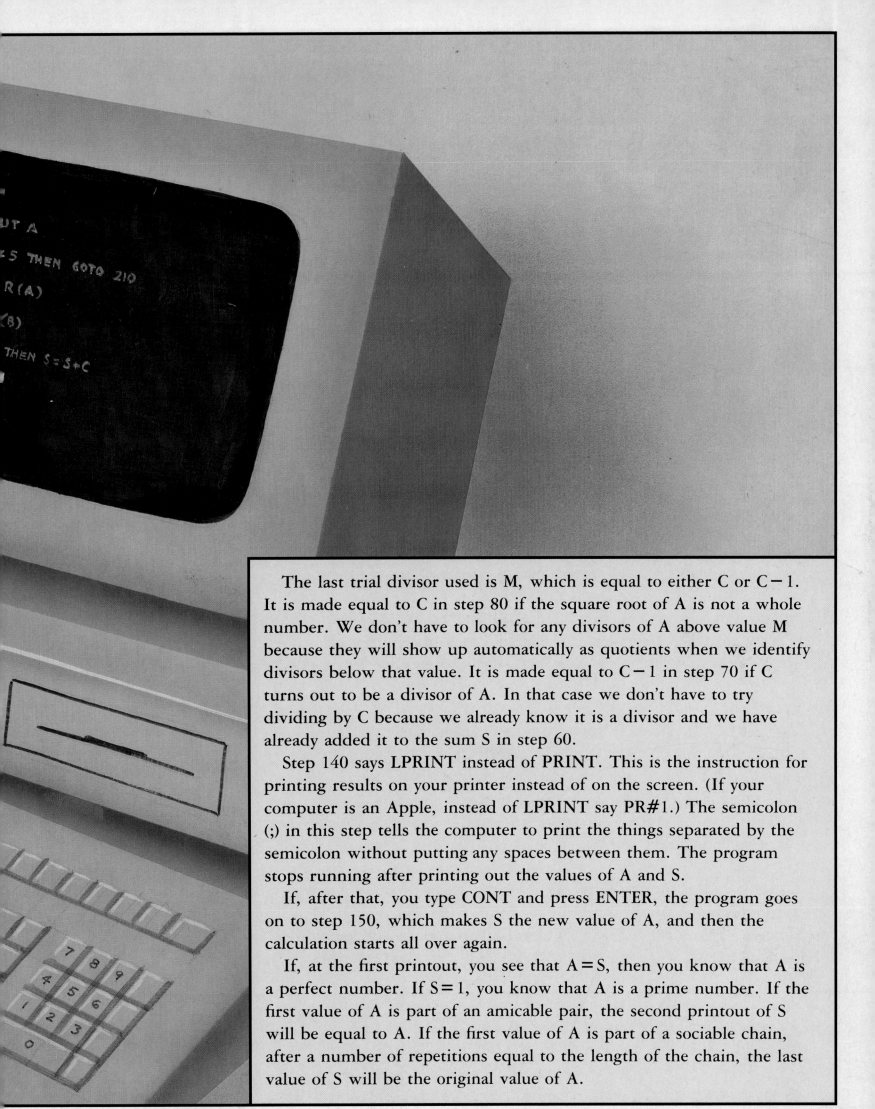

The last trial divisor used is M, which is equal to either C or C−1. It is made equal to C in step 80 if the square root of A is not a whole number. We don't have to look for any divisors of A above value M because they will show up automatically as quotients when we identify divisors below that value. It is made equal to C−1 in step 70 if C turns out to be a divisor of A. In that case we don't have to try dividing by C because we already know it is a divisor and we have already added it to the sum S in step 60.

Step 140 says LPRINT instead of PRINT. This is the instruction for printing results on your printer instead of on the screen. (If your computer is an Apple, instead of LPRINT say PR#1.) The semicolon (;) in this step tells the computer to print the things separated by the semicolon without putting any spaces between them. The program stops running after printing out the values of A and S.

If, after that, you type CONT and press ENTER, the program goes on to step 150, which makes S the new value of A, and then the calculation starts all over again.

If, at the first printout, you see that A=S, then you know that A is a perfect number. If S=1, you know that A is a prime number. If the first value of A is part of an amicable pair, the second printout of S will be equal to A. If the first value of A is part of a sociable chain, after a number of repetitions equal to the length of the chain, the last value of S will be the original value of A.

Fibonacci Numbers

In the year 1202 the book *Liber Abaci*, written by Leonardo Fibonacci of Pisa, introduced Arabic numerals to Europe. In the same book Leonardo had a puzzle problem about an imaginary population explosion of rabbits. Here is the problem: Suppose you start with a pair of newborn rabbits, one male and one female, and they produce one pair of rabbits, also male and female, at the end of two months, and another pair every month after that. Suppose, too, that each new pair does the same: They produce their first pair when they are two months old, and then produce another pair every month thereafter. Assume that this goes on forever. How many pairs of rabbits will there be at the beginning of each month?

Here is how to solve the problem: At the beginning of the first month there is 1 pair, the original pair. At the beginning of the second month there is still only 1 pair. At the beginning of the third month, when they have produced their first pair of babies, there are 2 pairs.

After that the pairs of rabbits at the beginning of any month will be made up of two parts. One part will be the rabbits who were already there the month before. So the number of pairs in this part is the number of pairs that existed the month before.

The other part will be the rabbits just born then. In this part there is one pair of baby rabbits for each pair of parents who gave birth. All these parents, being two months old or older, are precisely the pairs that already existed two months before. So the number of pairs in this part is the number of pairs that existed two months before.

Therefore, to find the number of pairs at the beginning of any of these later months, simply add the numbers of pairs that existed one month before and two months before.

The numbers obtained in this way, month after month, are now known as the *Fibonacci numbers*. We already know the first three of them: 1, 1, and 2. To get the rest, use the rule that you *add the last two to get the next one*. Therefore the next one is $1+2=3$; the next one after that is $2+3=5$; the next one is $3+5=8$, and so on. This then is the series of Fibonacci numbers: 1, 1, 2, 3, 5, 8, 13, 21, 34, 55, 89, 144, 233, etc.

To write a computer program for printing the first twenty Fibonacci numbers, let A, B, and C stand for the numbers in any consecutive triple. The program then must use the fact that the first values for A and B are both 1, and that $C=A+B$. The program is on the next page.

In this program, N stands for the position of each number in the series. The symbol F(N) stands for the Fibonacci number in the N'th position, and we read it as "F of N." $F(1)=1$, $F(2)=1$, $F(3)=2$, $F(4)=3$, $F(5)=5$, $F(6)=8$, and so on.

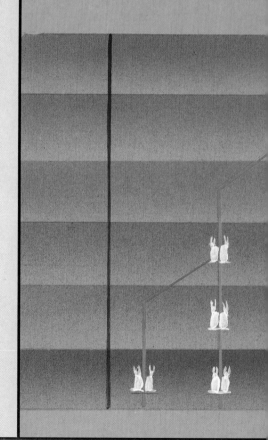

```
0 A = 1:B = 1:N = 2
0 PRINT A:PRINT B
0 C = A + B:N = N + 1
0 IF N = 21 THEN STOP
0 PRINT C
0 A = B:B = C:GOTO 40
```

There is an interesting property of Fibonacci triples that we will now discover. The table below lists the triples in order: The first triple begins with the first Fibonacci number, the second triple begins with the second number, the third triple begins with the third number, and so on.

If we call the middle number of any triple $F(N)$, then the number before it in the triple is $F(N-1)$, and the number after it in the triple is $F(N+1)$. The triples are in the second column of the table.

The third column contains the product of the first and third members of the triple. The fourth column contains the square of the middle number (the middle number times itself). The first column tells the position of the middle number of the triple in the Fibonacci series.

N	$F(N-1), F(N), F(N+1)$	$[F(N-1)] \times [F(N+1)]$	$[F(N)]^2$
2	1, 1, 2	2	1
3	1, 2, 3	3	4
4	2, 3, 5	10	9
5	3, 5, 8	24	25
6	5, 8, 13	65	64
7	8, 13, 21	168	169
8	13, 21, 34	442	441

On a piece of paper continue this table for two more lines, using the next two triples, 21, 34, 55, and 34, 55, 89. Do you see how the numbers in the third and fourth columns are related to each other? The answer is printed below upside down.

Answer: They differ by one. For even values of N, the third column is one more than the fourth column. For odd values of N, it is one less.

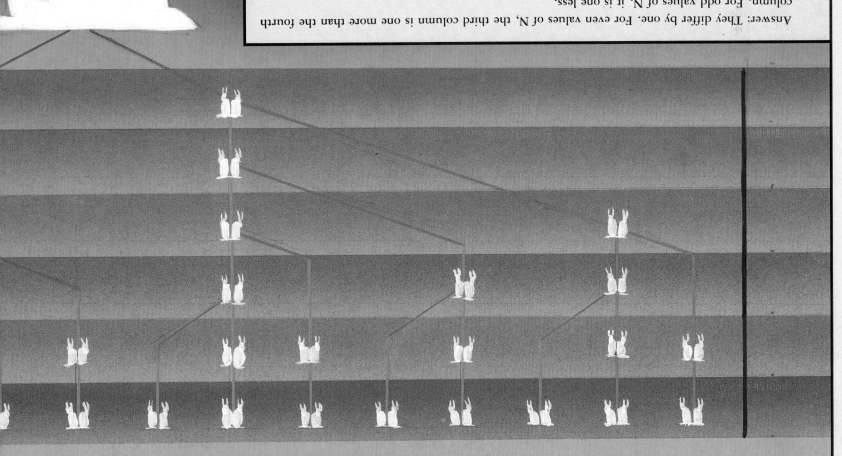

Plant Spirals and Fibonacci Numbers

One of the surprising and intriguing things about the Fibonacci numbers is that they occur in nature. If you look at a pineapple, you will see that its florets are arranged in two sets of spirals. One set of spirals goes up to the right. The other goes up to the left. The numbers of spirals in the two sets are usually 8 and 13, which are consecutive Fibonacci numbers.

There are similar spirals on an asparagus tip, a pine cone, and a sunflower head. On an asparagus tip, the numbers are likely to be 3 and 5; on a common pine cone, 5 and 8; on a large pineapple, 13 and 21; and on a sunflower, 34 and 55.

Such spirals are also found at the growing tip of a stem where the newly formed leaves are found before they grow long and separate. In nearly all cases, the numbers of spirals are consecutive Fibonacci numbers.

To see this for yourself, count the spirals on a pineapple or a pine cone. On a pineapple, first put a pin into a floret. Start your count with the spiral the pin is in that goes up to the right. Then count the spirals parallel to this one, each farther to the right around the pineapple, until you get back to the pin. Do not count the spiral with the pin a second time. Then count the spirals that go up to the left, again starting at the pin.

Botanists have proposed several different theories to explain why Fibonacci numbers occur on plants. This author has proved that they must occur if the distance between neighboring leaves, scales, or florets becomes as large as possible early in their growth.

Counting the Ancestors of a Male Bee

Another interesting occurrence of the Fibonacci numbers is in the number of ancestors a male bee has in each generation going backward in time. It is based on the fact that while a female bee grows from a fertilized egg, so that it has both a mother and a father, a male bee develops from an unfertilized egg, so that it has a mother but no father.

The chart on this page shows several generations of ancestors of a male bee. The parents of each generation are shown in the line above it. M stands for male. F stands for female. The number of bees in each generation is shown at the right. The numbers are all Fibonacci numbers in their proper order.

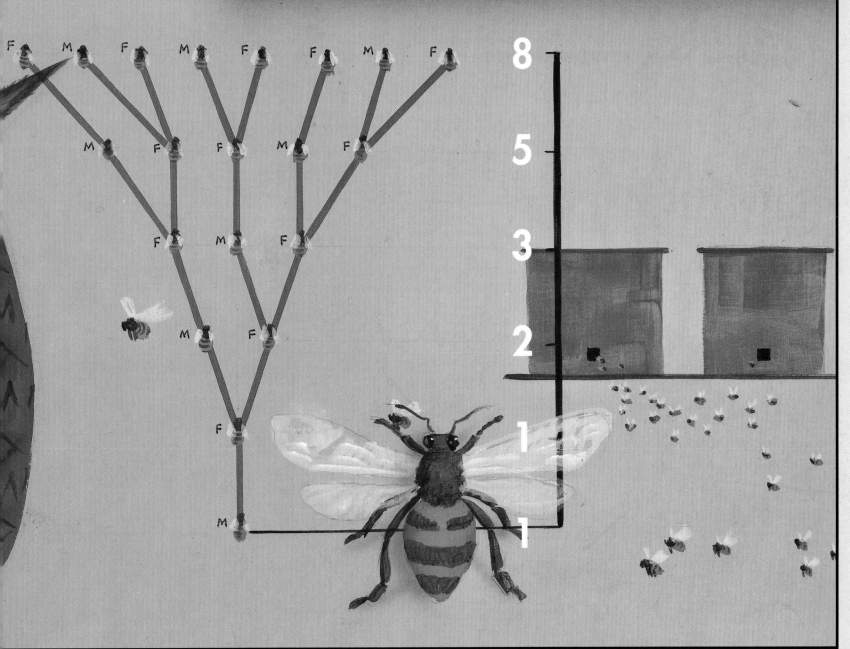

Regular Polygons

A *regular* polygon is one whose sides are equal and whose angles are equal. A regular polygon with three sides is called an *equilateral triangle*. Since the sum of the angles of a triangle is 180 degrees, each angle of an equilateral triangle contains 60 degrees (180/3).

A regular polygon with four sides is called a square. Since the sum of the angles of a four-sided polygon is 360 degrees, each angle of a square contains 90 degrees (360/4).

Each angle of a regular pentagon, which has five sides and whose angles add up to 540 degrees, contains 108 degrees (540/5). Each angle of a regular hexagon, which has six sides and whose angles add up to 720 degrees, contains 120 degrees (720/6).

If N stands for the number of sides in a regular polygon and A stands for the number of degrees in each of its angles, then A = $180 \times (N - 2)/N$. The computer program below calculates A for values of N from 3 to 20.

```
10 PRINT "N","A"
20 FOR N=3 TO 20
30 A=180*(N-2)/N
40 PRINT N,A
50 NEXT N
```

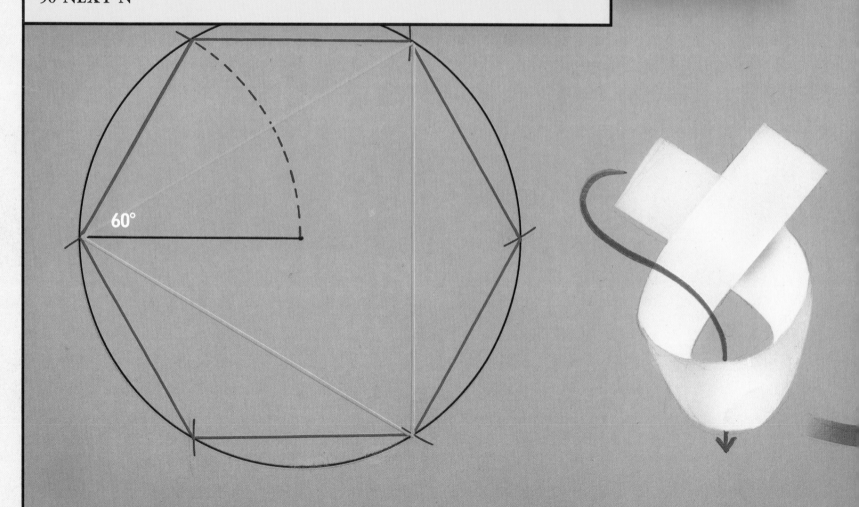

60°

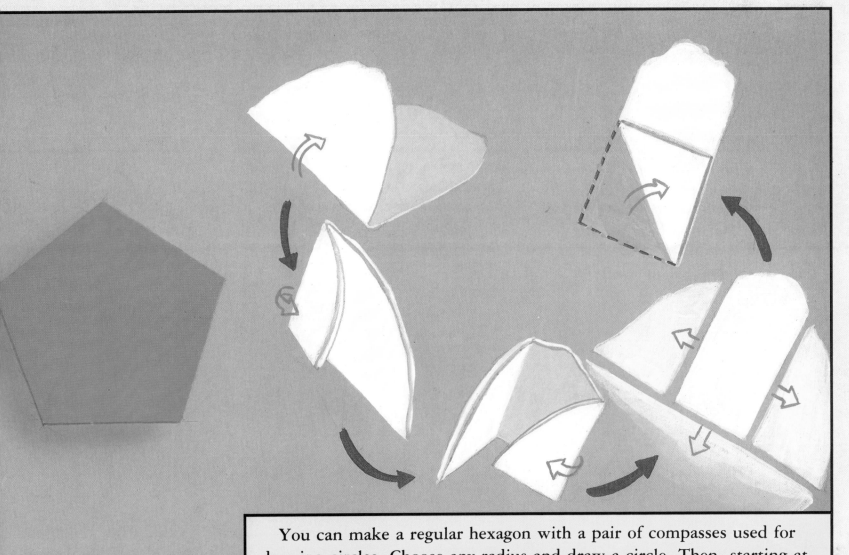

You can make a regular hexagon with a pair of compasses used for drawing circles. Choose any radius and draw a circle. Then, starting at any point on the circle, use the same radius to find a point on the circle whose distance from the starting point is equal to the radius. Use that point as the starting point and repeat the procedure. Keep going around the circle in this way, dividing it into equal arcs. At the end of the sixth arc you will be back where you started from. Now draw straight lines to join the six points that separate the arcs. The result is a regular hexagon. If you join each point to the second one away from it the result is an equilateral triangle.

You can make a square by folding paper, even if the paper you start with has no straight lines on its edge. Fold the paper once to get a straight line. Fold it again as described on page 20 to get a right angle on that line. Now fold it a third time to get a right angle at another point on that line. Cut the paper at the second and third creases. Now fold the paper for a fourth time, as described on page 20, to make a square.

You can make a regular pentagon by tying a knot in a strip of paper. Cut a narrow strip of paper so that it has the same width throughout its length. Bring one end of the strip over the other to form a loop. Then tuck the upper end inside the loop. Pull the two ends of the strip gently as far as you can without making the paper crumple. Three creases will form. Flatten the creases. The three creases and the other two sides of the knot form a regular pentagon.

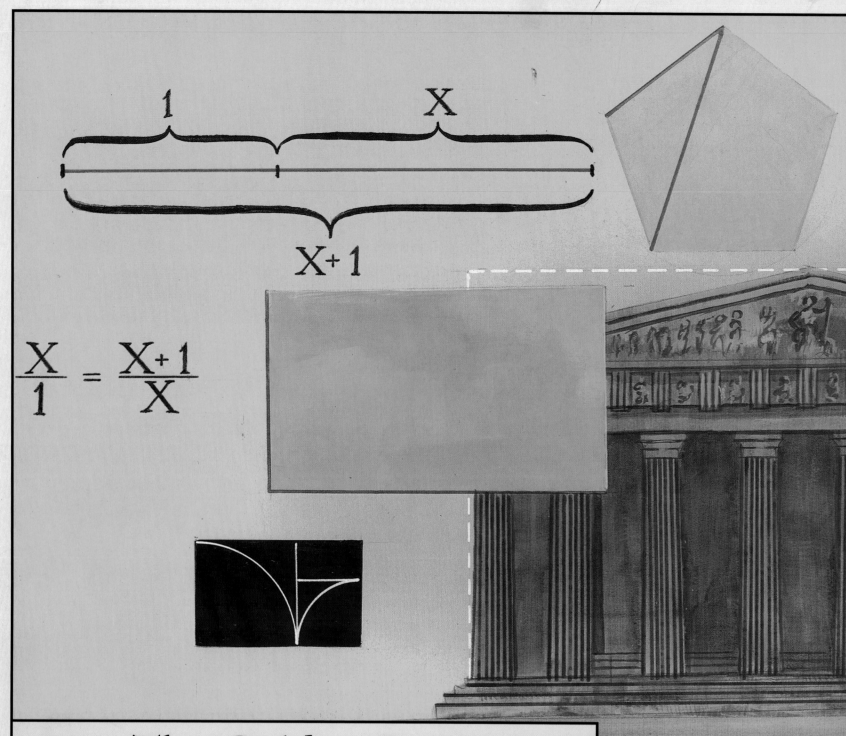

$$\frac{X}{1} = \frac{X+1}{X}$$

The Golden Ratio

The ratio of two lines is the length of one divided by the length of the other. Ever since ancient times people have been fascinated by one particular ratio known as the *golden ratio*. If you divide a line into two unequal parts, so that the ratio of the longer part to the smaller part is the same as the ratio of the whole line to the larger part, then that ratio is the golden ratio.

If the length of the smaller part is 1, and the length of the longer part is called x, then x is the golden ratio. The definition just given means that x/1 = (x + 1)/x. When this equation is solved, we find that x is one half the sum of 1 plus the square root of 5. Its value is approximately 1.618. It can be shown that the ratio of a diagonal of a regular pentagon to a side of the pentagon is the golden ratio.

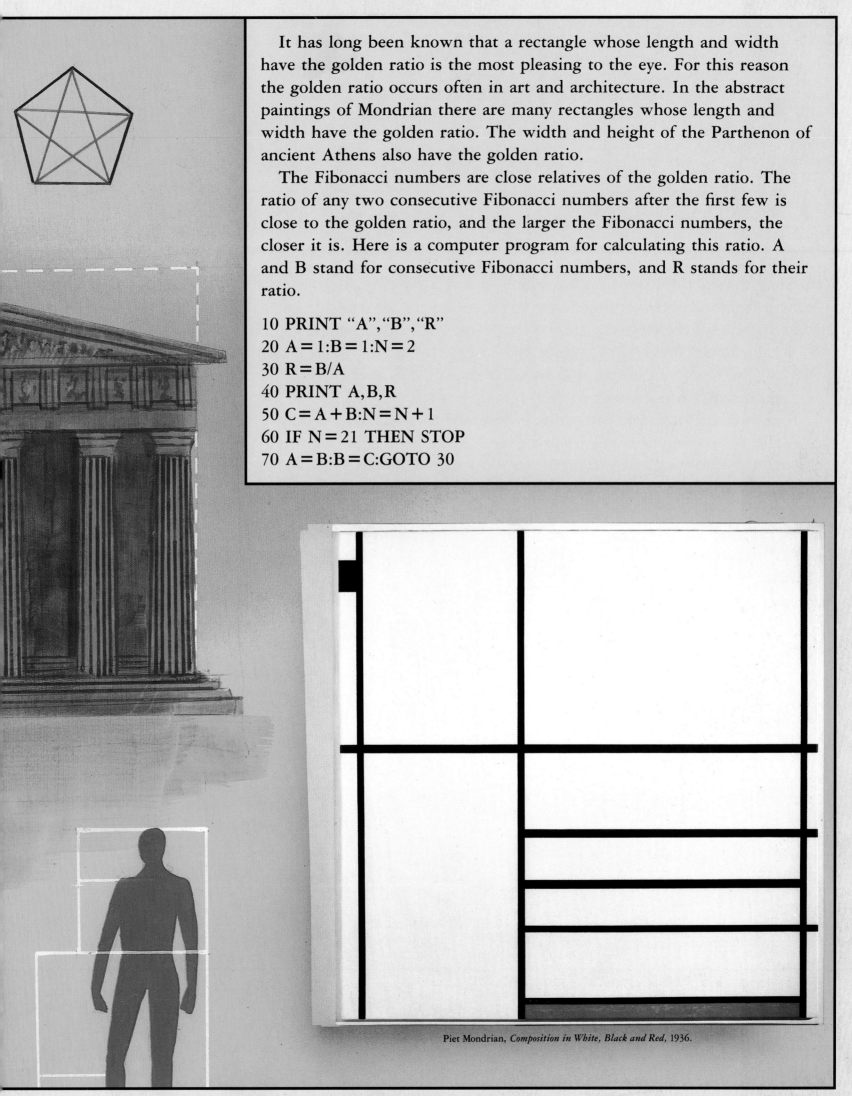

It has long been known that a rectangle whose length and width have the golden ratio is the most pleasing to the eye. For this reason the golden ratio occurs often in art and architecture. In the abstract paintings of Mondrian there are many rectangles whose length and width have the golden ratio. The width and height of the Parthenon of ancient Athens also have the golden ratio.

The Fibonacci numbers are close relatives of the golden ratio. The ratio of any two consecutive Fibonacci numbers after the first few is close to the golden ratio, and the larger the Fibonacci numbers, the closer it is. Here is a computer program for calculating this ratio. A and B stand for consecutive Fibonacci numbers, and R stands for their ratio.

```
10 PRINT "A","B","R"
20 A=1:B=1:N=2
30 R=B/A
40 PRINT A,B,R
50 C=A+B:N=N+1
60 IF N=21 THEN STOP
70 A=B:B=C:GOTO 30
```

Piet Mondrian, *Composition in White, Black and Red*, 1936.

The Growth of Mathematics

Mathematics is not a finished subject. As new needs arise in the work people do, new branches of mathematics are created to meet these needs.

In ancient times priests studied the motions across the sky of the sun, moon, and stars to be able to predict the changes of the seasons. Navigators crossing seas and oceans also looked to the sky for the stars that guided them. To help them in this work *trigonometry*, which relates distances to directions, was invented. In later centuries, when commerce grew rapidly around the Mediterranean Sea, there were calculations that had to be repeated often with new numbers each time they were done. To save time, ways of doing many problems all at once were invented. This was the beginning of *algebra*.

As commerce, industry, and science continued to develop, two kinds of problems kept coming up over and over again. One was to calculate the exact speed at a single instant in time of a moving object (a ball thrown through the air, for example). The other was to calculate the area inside a closed curve (the orbit of the earth, for example). A new branch of mathematics called *the calculus* was invented to solve these problems.

Sometimes a new branch of mathematics is created merely to satisfy the curiosity of the mathematician. Then a use for it may be found later. This is what happened with the *theory of numbers*. It was developed first merely to explore the properties of whole numbers. But it now has an important use in *cryptography*, the science of writing and breaking secret codes.

The growth of mathematics will never end. When new needs arise in the future, perhaps *you* will help to create the new mathematics that will meet these needs.

Index

About the Author

Dr. Irving Adler has had a distinguished career as a teacher, author, and scientist. He was chairman of the mathematics department at Textile High School in New York City and has taught math at Columbia University and Bennington College. He is the author of fifty-five books on mathematics, science, and education and co-author of many others, but is probably best known for his popular series of mathematics workbooks. Numerous books of his have been cited by the National Science Teachers Association and the Children's Book Council as "outstanding science books for children." Dr. Adler has also made important contributions in the field of mathematical biology. He now lives with his wife in North Bennington, Vermont.

About the Illustrator

Ron Miller worked for several commercial art studios before joining the Smithsonian National Air and Space Museum as the art director of the Albert Einstein Spacearium. After leaving the museum he opened his own art studio, from which he produces astronomical and science fiction illustration. Mr. Miller is a founding member of the International Association of Astronomical Artists, a member of NASA's Fine Arts Program, and a contributor to the National Commission on Space and NASA's Solar System Exploration Committee. He lives in Virginia with his wife.

EARLY MAN

MATHEMATICS WAS INVENTED BY OUR EARLIEST ANCESTORS
TO KEEP TRACK OF THE SEASONS AND TO TALLY BELONGINGS.

EUCLID

EUCLID WAS AN ANCIENT GREEK MATHEMATICIAN
WHOSE BOOK IS THE BASIS OF THE STUDY OF GEOMETRY.